Professional Love II

by

ADRIAN T. MARTIN

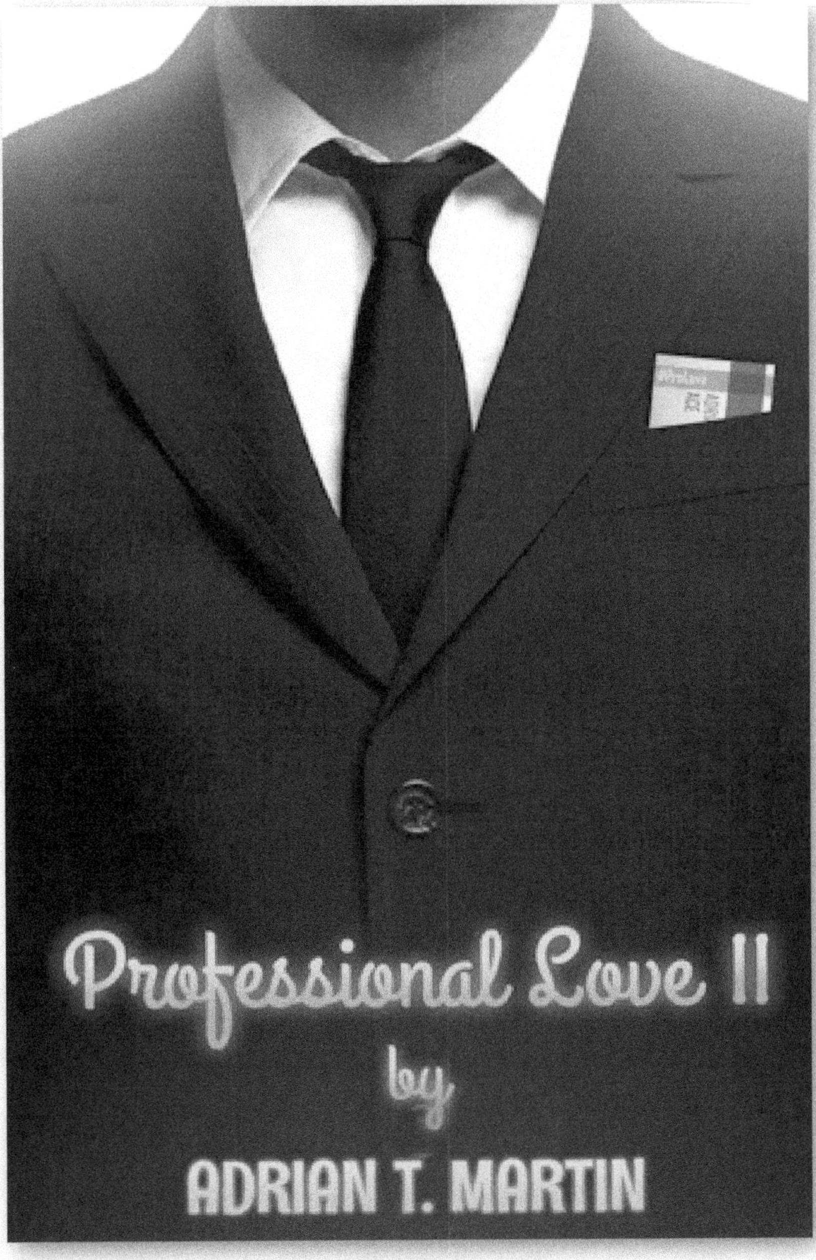

Professional Love II

Hughes Views

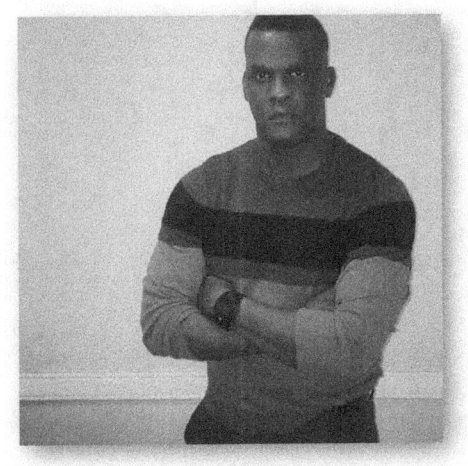

Adrian Ace Martin

© 2017 by Adrian Ace Martin
ISBN 13: 9780692953525
ISBN: 0692953523
Library of Congress Control Number: 2016912158
True Warrior Family, Montgomery, AL

Ordering Information

Special discounts are available on quantity purchases by corporations, associations, and
others. For details or purchases, contact the publisher at ace_martin_t@yahoo.com.
Orders by US trade bookstores and wholesalers available and open.
Printed in the United States of America.

Hughes Views is all about ones perspective

To Sharon Watkins and Johnny Grace:
without your love, none of this would be possible.

Professional (/prəˈfeSH(ə)n(ə)l/)

1. Relating to or connected with a profession.
2. A person engaged or qualified in a profession.

Love (/ləv/)

1. An intense feeling of deep affection.
2. Feeling a deep romantic or sexual attachment to (someone).

Hughes (/hjuːz/)

1. Of Germanic origin; *Hugo.*
2. Means "bright in mind and spirit" or "intelligence."

Open your heart;
love will find its way.

Table of Contents

Professional Love II

The love of writing is thrilling and exciting
I pray my thoughts are enticing
In writing, I limit tongue biting
In search of my dreams, I'm constantly fighting
Highlighting my history of events With handwriting
Passionate thoughts limit the ability of those who seek backbiting
On this road, I've endured storms and violent lighting
This love of being professional has turned confessional, obsessional, and successional
Can I possibly be as great as I think I am when it comes to love?
Am I Michael Jackson bad when he puts on the "Billie Jean" glove?
My thoughts are even more elevated as
I leave the audience fascinated with orchestrated, decorated, unregulated, rehabilitated, emancipated, and authenticated emotions
I aspire to a level of greatness that makes dreams come true
While also expiring the gun firing
I want you to dream bigger than life
And make your dreams a way of life
We rush home and drink all night, scared to face the bright lights
Dreams keeping us up at night
But we resist while following the social norm, which over time causes us mental harm
The thoughts weigh heavy with those who say "should've," "could've," and "would've"
But fear made couldn't

I leap on unsafe faith in hopes of self-fulfillment and, who knows, maybe a Rolls-Royce wraith

I hope you find love in all you attempt to do and that it's true to you

I hope your dreams come true

I hope you find your favorite hue of you

My thoughts provide a visual representation of blues

Too much booze, cuts, and bruises, extravagant cruises

Hardships similar to Jews', tissues for those with issues

Ideas for tattoos and a lot of different hues and views

Wake up; there is no time to snooze

As long as you have professional love, you can't lose

Alarm Clock

I need you to assume the position of being my alarm clock when
it's time to do something
I hate that I have to get up with the busy people at six o'clock in
the morning, stretching and yawning
But I figured since you get to relax
And oftentimes I scratch your feet and back
That you would return the favor and do that
You know *that*
That special thing I like that gets my feet pedaling like I'm on a
bike
Brings me that feeling of accomplishment after a long hike
I want to wake up free and light like a kite
When I'm at the house, unfocused and not paying attention to
details, don't raise hell
Just be my alarm clock by saying or doing things well and right
Let's get together and lose time watching Nick at Nite
When I lose focus on my career or life, I'm going to need to hit
the snooze button
To recap things because life can happen all too sudden
Don't leave me behind like Joe Budden
Time showing things could have been but it wasn't
Let's forget about everything but you and me, capeesh?
Let's unplug and cease on the alarm-clock thing at least

Elevation (Howard Hughes)

Like Howard Hughes
Strategizing in a plane, his goal was to fly
To do that, he had to gain elevation and beyond
The clouds he found his freedom
In reality, he was a racist man with an
Eccentric lifestyle who hardly smiled
We all could argue if elevation
Freed him from the world that held him captive
In a way, regardless of what we believe in
If we find elevation, we can find difference
If you get an education
You will find that in society you have elevation
You no longer have to work at the bottom of the company—you're
at a higher ground
If your money increases, you rise above certain struggles and
those in it—that is elevation
If you become as powerful as a president or a king, you will sit
higher than the rest of the people because it's about elevation
We all should want to elevate
So *elevate*!

Lauryn

Born in New Jersey with talents that would soon give the world surgery
The Miseducation of Lauryn Hill
Has changed how most really feel
A young Queen they call "L. Boogie"—extremely talented with voice and lyrical content
Her persona is a collective tribute
Of what makes African Americans the best they could possibly be
Her music is a reflection of the hardships we face on a daily basis, including the issues with racists
We laugh and feel pain and sorrow as she sings about issues from the past, present, and tomorrow
Inspiring a new way of thinking—you would think she's the horseman from Sleepy Hollow
A true role model to follow for the urban community
Being a reflection of joy and unity
I find it hard to say that I would have peace of mind if she wasn't around
As a conquering lion, she gets out the mysteries of iniquity
Delivering positive waves that pull us out of misery
Liberated in thoughts and focused—I'd say Adrian doesn't live in theory
Consequently, constantly making me weary and sometimes teary
She has so much to say
Listeners find freedom from war in mind

She helps to release chains of social binds
At least a decade ahead of time
Ready or not, here she comes
To impact lives and make a difference, being free in mind, gifted
and kind

From a Distance

From a distance, I admire your infinite
Beauty and wisdom
Your grace is remarkable
With a twist of aggression
The energy you have elevates a
Woman to a height that is indescribable
Yet it looks good and feels good all at the same time to see you
elegantly move
Just knowing your actions are true
Real to what you are, what you try to be, and what others should
be is an accolade
You spend most of your time focused on self-improvement, and
when you're not, you're improving others
You don't rely on your buttocks or chest; instead, you face life,
giving everything your best
I don't know you, and I barely know your name, and some say
life's about risk; well, I'm ready to play the game
To show you to my family and friends would be more than about
the beauty of your skin
It would be more about how we faced challenges, and to add to
conquering or victories, I found you, which exceeds a win
Most men chase women of vanity, which puts them on the brink
of sanity
Not having a queen on a throne
Or an honor like a Grammy

No grace just fille de joie
Who switch up like weather in Miami
Frustrated conversations about
"When are you going to come home?"
I see from a distance that you are more beautiful than any star in
the sky
If given the chance I'd be the perfect guy
To close the distance

Judas

I show you the light
You push me into darkness
I give you directions
And you try to get there without me
Not realizing I'm the one with the keys to
Open the gate, which yields success and treasures that are unseen
Now that you've arrived, your trip was worthless
Was the deceit worth it?
Staring at failure
I bet you feel right at place
Toward me, you manifest hate or hold aggression, when in reality
I just
Wanted to be your protection
I'd do anything to take you with me
And you'd do anything to make it alone with all the glory unearned
I thought we were brothers in the same struggle
Facing the same problems from day to day
You would do anything for at least a dollar in extra pay
We travel together, but for the love of diamonds, you'd push me
into the Colosseum to fight bears and lions
Holding steel or iron, I look up crying, but my strength comes
from Zion
Difference is you got the tendencies of Judas
I got faith and ambition in God
I showed you all the love I had in my heart

And you leave me abandoned and cold like Walmart shopping carts

In troubled times, I face adversity like a gladiator; you cower in hiding but emerge for credit after the war and achieved victory

I'm the blame for all that is bad

But when all is well, you claim to have been around

But the whole time you were busy trying to take me down

Do I appear to be stupid or look like a clown?

I give you bread and wine

You exposed all my secrets, and as I fall down, bleeding out, hurting, and dying

You're laughing as my executioner says I'm charged for slander and lying

Just know I no longer live in your world

But in the future watch out for me

I'm about to glow

Forever in the light

Nickels and Dimes

Born into America and its culture, we as citizens want success so much it's menacing

We work at jobs, acquiring nickels and dimes in hopes we will get ahead of times

Many of us run from scenes of crimes

In endangered times

With elevation stuck on our minds, we become blind

To our communities, which are full of the crimes

Greed triggers illegitimate activities like snorting white lines and cocking nines

You drive a Benz but want a Rolls-Royce to the

Point it might cause you a divorce

She already cut back on the sexual intercourse

So please be there for her, show some remorse, and support

Too often we buy things we can't afford to impress people we don't like

Putting us farther behind on the chase of nickels and dimes

Life's a climb, so if you have such a long way to go, why boast near the base floor

You just got to prove to God

You're worthy of heaven

Not to the world; you bust MAC-11s, that you real, or that you trill

On the climb, be persistent and focused in mind

Believing you can accomplish the toughest goals while keeping everything else in line

That's the people who talk down on you, that's that crazy job, that's the folks who put dirt on your name, that's anything that can deter your mission

Face your intuition; good fish and chicken belong in the kitchen

With confidence in self, you can be an honorable mention

Stop the penny-pinching, learn and understand your goals, nickels, and dimes

Which, in time, will become success and dollar signs

Beyoncé

I can only imagine how you feel
Focusing on your craft and keeping it real
You're so talented that your minor mistakes are a big deal
Do you live in a glass box where
Critics always have so much to say when you move closer toward
your goals and dreams everyday
Since a young age, you have possessed a God-given talent and cata-
pulted to the top of our generation and culture, despite the criti-
cism and hate
At least a decade of positivity and love when given frustration and
hate
An icon of our time
Fighting for the empowerment of young black girls and women
alike, inspiring personalities to win independently instead of
depending
With every single you release, they claim it's something else rath-
er than gifted
Moving unscripted, your actions
Keep us lifted
I ask who's the best, and they try everything to resist saying you
run the world
Word to the BeyHive
You're as gifted as Michael when he came from the Jackson 5
Used to ball with the Texas swag
Wearing your hat low or to the side like "Hovito"

Your music chills my soul below subzero

You're our Wonder Woman without a rope or an invisible plane

Your voice is "Purple Rain"

Stimulating our heart and brains

I don't understand why all can't see how beautiful you really are

You're so amazing, Mona Lisa doesn't event compare

When you move we are compelled to stop and stare

As a young male teen who found love, I reminisce and think back how "Dangerous in Love" was our soundtrack

They say a lot of crazy things, but your mark on the world, they can never take that

People sometimes party for a B-day, bringing out a formation, feeling Sasha Fierce while sipping lemonade and dangerously falling in love

But you inspired them to wait a while

Just by listening to the emotions of Destiny's Child

You are the greatest, and as long as you're here, we hope to see you smile

Naïve Individual Glorifying Greed and Encouraging Racism

Such an issue that has to be discussed
We as Afro-Americans see a lot of niggers
I feel subject to classism
I know it's wrong to speak in this perspective
Or talk down, but maybe the message will get around that we
need less niggers spelled with an *r*
N.E.G.U.S is for young Kings and Queens
Niggers is for the thots and idiots on TV screens
Shows misleading youth, poisoning our communities
Inspiring hatred not unity
Niggers killing negus
Our goal is to make a life for ourselves and our people until a
nigga who thinks he's making the right decision breaks into our
houses, rapes our women, shames our ancestors, brings down ev-
eryone, creates drug addictions
Shames our race, decreases our space in society, destroys the in-
terpretation of role models, disregards God, and inspires eccen-
tricity and oddness
Don't let the people you love lose sight of goals and dreams; to
find God and inspire should be the focus
Don't be blinded by the love of the cream
Accomplish your dreams but still
Have love

It's not black on black
It's niggers on black
But with all that said, I still got love for my niggers

Scared to Fly (Langston Hughes)

What happens to those who are scared to fly?

Do they fear
Reaching for higher altitude?
Do they have the may-crash attitude
And never try?
Do they let criticism destroy their will to fly?
Do they go after their hopes to
Peace and serenity?

Maybe they just give up
On touching the sky?

Or do they actually fly?

She Got Kids

I like her, but damn, she got kids
I wonder if she a thot or if she get it open
For any dude with cash or benefits
I heard the last guy she was with wasn't ish
He was cruel, tortured and hit her
Often he'd forget her
Told her she would never be ish
Especially since she got kids
I heard she's a very educated and hardworking young lady; I don't
have any doubts, but damn, she got kids
She might be the one, but nah, she got kids
Considering if we do try
I got to take her and all her badass kids to showbiz
I really don't know if I can handle all them damn kids
She fell victim to a waste man
So I don't know if I can be the best man
They say if a woman has moved around
It ain't a good sign
That she might not be able to keep a man, but who knows, maybe
she has better plans
But...
As of lately, I been feeling some type of way
I been feeling like I don't give a damn
If she got kids, she's beautiful, so it is what it is

I like the woman she is; I like how she carries herself, and god-
damn it, I even see *God* in her eyes
Body of a goddess with pretty brown eyes and peanut butter thighs
I don't care about her past or other guys
She's the best thing in my eyes
Besides, who am I to judge?
Especially when I'm not picture perfect
I believe it's worth it
I'm willing to jump into a relationship
Unlike lesser men, I see she doesn't fall
Into the stereotype
She got her mind right and her body right and
Her conversations give me light
Thinking of her, I can't sleep at night
I guess we all going to showbiz
Because I don't give a damn if she got kids!

I Got Tired

I got tired of being in need
I got tired of seeing others succeed
Especially when I know I can exceed
I got tired of not getting my chance
I got tired of my circumstances
I got tired of not being able to provide
I got tired of being pushed aside
I got tired of being hungry
I got tired of asking, "Can I borrow gas money?"
I got tired of saying, "I'll pay you on Sunday."
I got tired of borrowing money
I got tired of depending on others
So I found the courage and energy to do better and be like no other
Now I don't get tired

Timeline

The test of time shows me where we stand
Not just my Facebook timeline
The times I did something great, instead of saying, "I'm proud of you," you'd say, "How did you do it?"
More concerned primarily with what you could do to do it better instead of pushing or supporting me
The times I got in trouble with people or the law, it was more of a humorous event than a struggle in your eyes
I spent a large amount of time down and out, and only by the grace of God did I find my way out and toward a better day
My ideals or contributions to the world
You adopted as your own goals; by watching me, you kind of figured if you do what I do then you might become successful or have an idea on what to do
When I have conversations with people who may know things, you devalue my words
And try to win their favor for no reason
Anytime I did anything, I realized you found poisonous thoughts or words to bring forth
When I was dealing with pressure
If I had a ruler, it wouldn't be much to measure how much you helped
When I needed you most
You just drifted away like a riverboat
I realize people change with time
On that note, I've made up my mind to remove you from my timeline

Warrior King Dream

Last night I had a dream I was a warrior king
Who freed and liberated people
Lethal as Steven Seagal
Intimidating as Beanie Sigel
Swords, knives, and arrows
With visions of a sparrow
Giving hope to people of Sierra Leone
I never claimed to be king, but it's just so
I took the seat on the throne
My barbaric scent was the best cologne
Such heroic actions are why I've never been seen to do wrong
Helping to carve out destinies for those who are unable to reciprocate energy
Destroying slave masters who rape, hate, distort our history, and keep our people in deep misery
Young radicals with methods that are mathematical
Providing for families and community, living with diplomatic immunity, above the law for all I've done, including inspiring unity
Women get in lines to let me see their curves and design
Me selecting them based on vanity; when you king in those times, it's all physical, so a great derriere is a major key, especially when you freeballing and got victories like Ginóbili
Every day as king, I destroy physical and mental chains that limit those who are able to be great
Such a feeling of ecstasy

It could have been a movie or a wet dream
Similar to *Game of Thrones* where I rule over the seven kingdoms
Beheading Prince Joffrey, and those to the likes of Littlefinger
The celebration of freedom consist of slaying the social beast, flowers at my feet, a royal feast, and a queen fucking me drunkenly to sleep

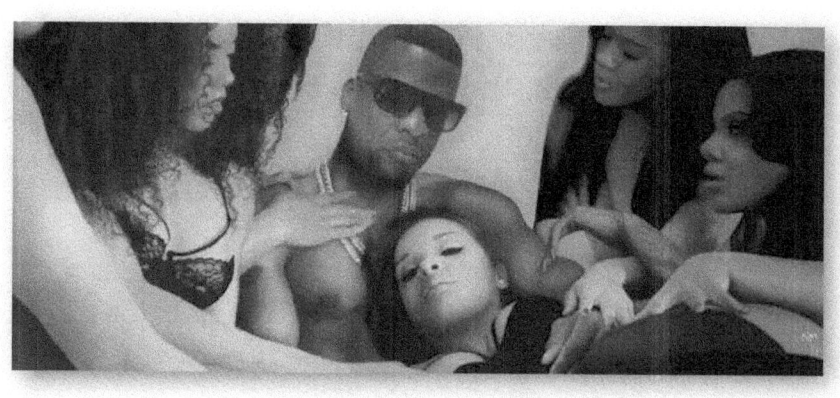

I Don't Give a Damn

I just don't give a damn what they say about me
I want to be with you
I understand you made mistakes
And everyone knows about them
I understand you got kids and the daddy ain't around
But if I love you I'll be around; how do I sound, leaving you down
When I know what I feel is real
I won't complain or make a big deal
I don't give a damn that you made mistakes in your past
I care about who you are today and where your heart stands
How can I be a positive example for young men
When it's all about the size of an ass rather than character or class
of a woman
I don't know what the issue is, but I know how I feel
And I know it's real
I don't give a damn about your ex-man
Because I believe I'm the best man
I don't give a damn about what people say
You only brighten up my day
Too many people dwell on past circumstances and miss out on the
perfect romance or opportunity
I don't give a damn about your downfalls
Because we all fall
I just hope you give me your all

And we can start to crawl and eventually learn to fly
I don't give a damn because I know you're the one
And I'm the perfect guy

A Million

I'd rather die than live my life as a coward
I'd rather fail a million times before I decide to be a quitter
I'd rather be making a difference than be out here beefing and killing
I'd rather not have children than be a man who doesn't take care of his family
A million people will be followers, but I will be that leader
A million mistakes can be made, but I'll make the decision to save millions
A million people will doubt me, but it only takes him to believe in me

Muhammad

As a young kid, I was found in the streets, trying to survive and
stand on my feet

I avoided trouble, grew, and learned to respect authority, while
also comprehending history

I slowly started to understand priorities and why we are known
as the minority

Why others see themselves as superiority, when in actuality they
are cowards with the luck of being the absolute majority

Fighting my whole life, I decided I might as well step into a ring at
the age of twelve and show the world the strength of fallen kings

I am a humble individual with the best intentions if you look and
listen; my heart is filled with love and forbearing, but you're hate-
ful and demanding

At the age of eighteen, I'm awarded the title as a light heavyweight
Olympian, so I could promise you a crash landing, but in life I'm
more into mind expanding and looking to be upstanding

Avoiding your stigmatizing or branding me of being another naive
individual glorifying greed and encouraging racism

I found myself frustrated in 1960, returning from Rome as a
champion and still being refused service, wondering what the
purpose was and was it really worth it

I had the best feeling being called the greatest before I returned
home to see my people barely making it

I wear these medals all the time, but with tears in my eyes, I tossed them over Louisville Bridge because now I see things clearer
I am now more than Cassius Clay, but who is this man in the mirror?

Playboy (Hugh Hefner)

I can fuck hoes all night, or I can fall in love
Seems like falling in love is the better and typical answer
Truth is, I got trust issues with these women; several lied
And said they're having my children; truth is, they had multiple men
At least with the single women, I can brag to my friends
About how I live stress-free financially and like a king
Every night, the women hitting notes like Mariah
With several phone numbers, I'm fire; I know I'm the shit
I mean, look at me—I'm everything; I have beaten every statistic
I'm handsome, in shape, educated, and often imitated
What do they want? These whores want scholarships
Paid tuition and easy ways to advancement
As long as my phone stays ringing at night
My community will hear females singing
My spirit cries out for love
But to my knowledge it's nonexistent
So many adventures I can't count; what has become of me now?
Maybe I should settle down
Because when I look around, I'm lonely and always down
I don't want to be a player when you pull back the layers
Gravity is working against me like John Mayer, and I need a woman to be my Bayer
I realize the Playboy ish is what I accept because

I haven't found the right one who would treat me like a mayor
When the lights get low and you're tired of cutting everybody's
grass with your mow
You just have to know how to find the love below

God's Spy

What if birds were spies of God?
Flying low and reading our minds and hearts
Analyzing our struggles
Seeing whose well-off versus who's not
Singing for those who are humble and caring
And attacking the jerks of the world
What if birds just got close to us to hear our conversations
About where we stand in the nation?
What if birds were souls
Putting in overtime to make it into heaven?
What if birds were secretly angels watching over us?
Why are birds so mysterious?
What if your ancestors came back as birds, singing, scaring
And directing you on the correct path in life?
What if birds were spirits who got lost looking for love?
What if birds sing to you to show you they appreciate your char-
acter and beauty?
What would happen if we took the time
To realize something so small yet so beautiful as a bird?
What if being beautiful in life turns us into birds?

Kanye

I LOVE KANYE!
Late 2004 in English class
Our teacher told us to write about a poet that was monumental
or from the past
Being late from the computer lab
I make it to class with lyrics printed and written on my notepad
My collar is up, but I put it down
When I recited it all falls down
Everyone was quiet, and I didn't even hear a sound
Considering T.I. and Young Jeezy are the hottest around
I was an imitation in sound
Though the wire must've been underground
Because I spit it so superb and knew every word
I even scored the best—the teacher gave me a hundred on the test
that she placed on my desk
You touched my soul with "Jesus Walks" when critics talked; for
self-righteousness I fought
Your lyrics inspire me to have greatness in thought.
Because after "Killa Cam" came the slow jam
And then the Katrina dam
But you helped us deal with politicians and gold diggers; I even
heard you say we can touch the sky
Nothing's like the glory of a good morning of a good life
Because some days you will feel heartless in the coldest winters
while walking under streetlights

The power of all the lights will make you run away into the night
But as a knight you watch the throne because the world is full of new slaves and not the brave
In the ultralight beams, we are surrounded by wolves who wanna see us fade
An icon in my eyes; when you emerged you caught me by surprise
I relate to the passion of the art and the culture
And connect on the ideal of not dying without trying to inspire or make a difference
I pray for you from time to time because they say you lost your mind
I know your creativity exceeds and you're ahead of time
As a young brother, I could only imagine the pain of losing your mother
Simply because she can't be replaced by no other
As a younger brother, I pray you find the strength to go further
There will never be another
Kanye West, my big brother

It Makes Her Sad

It makes her sad to see me drinking and driving
Up to 3:30, sipping and riding dirty, not foreseeing the consequences of my situation
The outcome I could be facing is not sufficient and very degrading
It makes her sad to see me fussing and fighting with people who are undeserving of my recognition
It makes her sad that sometimes I don't listen and lose sight of my intuition
But like R. Kelly, she scorns my focus into ignition
Revitalized, I produce fresh out of the kitchen new and improved thought patterns
Darkness in thoughts like a cavern have been shattered
Was disoriented like I spent all night in a tavern
As a young man, I find focus on life; as a lover, I give the best advice
But it makes her sad to see me with multiple women instead of a wife
Kids and a wife would be nice, but I'm so free-spirited and enjoying more life
Nights are not steady, so love weighs on me
I'm usually lonely or dealing with beautiful women who too lazy to cook me some macaroni
I'm advised to find someone with relationship goals
To avoid the phony and those only seeking money
It makes her sad that I face real-life issues on a daily basis
And I keep them all inside; she says I got too much pride
It makes her sad that she's here to help but I push her aside

Millie

In you I found myself
I found complete happiness and understanding
I found that piece of me that makes me dream big and aspire to be better than yesterday
Even though everywhere I went from my neighborhood to school I was called out of my name
Which isn't cool
Outside of my immediate family
You supported me and understood my dreams, as well as growing pains
Standing up as a dreamer in my youth was a mental strain
Being creative makes normal people call you lame
That's just part of the game
Doing everything you can to make a difference
Creating magic like a magician
And people shoot you down in an instant
You inspired the best in me, and people
Tried to lock me down like I committed a felony
Despite our differences, you saw the gift and ambition in my melanin
You sought to water the thoughts in my melon
When us students traveled out of town on music trips, you took us by our hands
You treated us all equal, which is how it should be in the hearts of all men

I remember going places where some kid's family had extreme
wealth, and they turned their cheeks
Without having knowledge of self
Us kids just wanted to sing, but they mistook our passion as if we
needed help
You saw our frustrations and pain
You eased our will to complain
Mrs. Millie, you took us higher than any plane

One Day in the Gump

I hit the nightclub to take the stage
And make an impact in a community that lacks unity
I make my way to the restroom, heavily intoxicated, not noticeably drinking or frustrated
Lightly nervous, I see them thugs in the restroom as I assume to free the liquids that was coming to soon
They told me to get out because it's too many niggaz in the restroom
Seeing I'm surrounded, I keep my thoughts grounded, no matter how rude it looked or sounded
Making my way out, another brother entered and was greeted with the same approach, but he wasn't having it—he was looking for free smoke
My name is called to hit the stage, and I find motivation instead of rage
Once I hit the stage, those two individuals stumble across the club, fighting like "Streets of Rage"
I grab the mic and say, "Y'all cut out the nonsense—this we shouldn't do," and the DJ pulled my plug on stage and said, "Nobody knows you."
Embarrassed, shamed, and humiliated, I stand on the stage and chaos happens
The fight goes outside, and once again I go for the mic, since it started to calm down

All of a sudden, it sounded like we were hit by a bomb, as bullets hit the building and gunshots rained like we were at war with Saddam

I feared for my life and even thought of my mom

I ran back into the restroom, which seemed like the best room, but eventually it was too many niggaz in the room

Entering the restroom, I see glass crushed in a man's face as he was bleeding steady, his blood dripping red like cranberry; I had just come to rap for this——I wasn't ready

It was a nightmare in the gump, and by all means, I was trying to avoid Freddy

When the guns stopped, my friend came to the rescue

I was thinking, "Thank God it's you."

We ran out of the building in a complete panic; it was one of the two lying at the entrance of the club, holding on for his dear life

I went to work saddened because he died that night

Just one day in the gump

Just a Little Closer (From a Distance Part II)

Started off from a distance, but I was consistent
On covering ground and observing new territories
I had fears oftentimes you'd see me stumbling, fumbling, or dropping things
I had to find balance on my feet; I been around longer than Windcreek
Waiting for the right time to speak or be unique
I can't come closer by complimenting your physique because
I'd be saying the same things as undeserving men playing games
You know how I feel; I just hope you feel the same
I'm willing to take up to a year's time in search of your heart, mind, and being your man
I want us to grow like Rogaine and explode like propane
I'd do anything to win you over so I won't be down like Kurt Cobain
Singing "How to Love" like Lil Wayne at your windowpane
It's something about you that makes me sing
You're more beautiful than any jewel or diamond ring
I see you and I feel higher than planes; I lose all my will to complain; I'm speeding to you
In the fast lane, hoping I can catch you like the little choo-choo train or Jay Jay the Jet Plane.
I'm behind enemy lines, crawling in muddy terrain

Looking to my left and right, I see the other men I can't let capture you and win

I'm a veteran, so I will cross the burning sands and rescue you from evil hands

Don't fall for the Taliban; trust in GI Adrian the American

Your digits verify your location

So I'll be there if you believe in communication

As I get just a little closer, I see you're standing right where you're suppose too

Just a little closer

Sundress

The dawg comes out when I see the sundress on your beautiful
skin

As you flawlessly move through society, I'm flattered by your
existence

I hate to carry myself, thinking about what's on the outside versus
what's within

When I sip that hen, I think about getting it in

Elegantly and majestically, you move where any man who sees you

Has a feeling of hesitancy when it's time to talk

Because that sundress walk is hotter than a sunny-day sidewalk

You're thunderous in a sundress, holding powers of an Egyptian
goddess

You appear wondrous; staring at your lipstick, I lust for you as a
sidekick

If life's a game, you can play with my joystick

I'mma bad boy—take my nightstick; I'm just trying to figure you
out, and you're tougher than arithmetic

To win you over is like politics; will you ever jump the broomstick?

Am I wrong for just enjoying the thickness of a beautiful sundress
chick?

T-Shirt and Panties

Why you playing mind games with your man?
You know I'm staring at your fanny when you wear T-shirt and panties
You look better than any Grammy, you look hotter than Miami
We rendezvous in my bedroom, where neighbors know my name
And you only moan, scream, or cause a loud boom
Your sweet smell of Chanel takes me away from this life of hell from time to time
Buried under you, I find peace of mind
Your booty is a stress ball that when I squeeze relaxes me to my knees
When we make love, it sounds like a fighting movie in Chinese
So the nosey neighbors call the police; when they arrive, we just spray Febreze
Opening the front door, looking tired and greased, they just say, "Have a nice day, please."
Fuck 'em; the next time they knock, we won't answer the door, 'cause they ain't got no keys
I'm just trying to keep your legs shaking like Parkinson's disease
I can't believe all this; for me to see, you're as sexy as ever in your white tee and panties
I'm beyond freaky and mannish—I guess my weakness is your T-shirt and panties

You and Her

You gave me all your trust, and I comfort you
You help me define me in times of disaster or catastrophe
You defend me when opposers attempt to spread blasphemy
Unlike gravity, you don't work against me; we find joy and love rampantly
We vacay and bashfully align like stars in the galaxy as we embrace
On a midnight balcony, finally reaching our *Final Fantasy*
You look over my flaws and abnormalities, supporting me on my quests of philanthropy
When I take risks financially for hopes of advancements in humanity
This you defend with extraterritoriality, believing I'm right and everyone else
Is superficial; if they argue, you reign like a cavalry
But...*she*...well, she sees the best in me professionally
Stimulating me sexually, intellectually providing a challenge
Feeling like Sebastian from *Cruel Intentions*, I look for intervention
My heart is caught between two, seeking its apprehension
When she sees me, she wants it like a reciprocating engine, forcing me to spank her
And put her in detention, so I always forget to mention to her about her suspension
So I fall, weak to her heart, smile, and dimensions, a true obsession with retention

I need both of y'all love—can I get an extension? Damn, I had good intentions
They say you can't have cake and eat it too, but ain't that what you suppose to do?
About to crash on all this love; I got to hit the emergency brake
Before the waters run dry in my artificial lake or
I'll have to cry a river like Justin Timberlake
It can all come tumbling down like an earthquake, so before it's too late
I choose you, but who are you?

You Need Me

With intentions to isolate me and people like me
I kind of figured you must be intimidated by my presence
You started a business, and although you hate me, you depend on me
To enter so you can generate wealth and maintain your establishment
The items you sell cater to me and people like me; you got some nerve
Opening a business in my community, which you don't care for or about
My people need supplies, and they got to come to your store, knowing you hate them
It's shocking that you *aren't* assaulted or robbed
Being a culture vulture doesn't make you great or inspire memorial sculptures
Are you more focused on inspiring a generation, running the nation, or just making money?
Regardless what you choose, you still need me; without me, your business will fail
You could be homeless and depending on a community of people you don't like
In the darkest hour, you'll say to yourself, "They need me."

Marinate

I want us to marinate
I want to be with you like steak
At a tailgate, like cellphones on a first date
Or cops on *The First 48*
Even though I got twenty-one questions like 50 and Nate
Tell them haters to get to stepping
Like a Sigma probate
I can open doors windows and gates like Bill Gates
I envision us being soul mates, where our spirits marinate
In a full house like Ashley and Mary-Kate
Love stoned in my current state, when all I want to do is elevate
All I want is you now that he is gone
Being a friend is killing me softly
Don't push me away; there's no need to separate
Do you want to be interrogated? Because I feel alienated
To you I'm dedicated, giving all my time as if I'm an inmate
If I can't be yours and you be mine, tell me who to eliminate
I want us to be free, but not like the confederates
My thoughts are on us and how I have seen our love originate
On those thoughts, I meditate
Until we have ate, accelerate, educate, and understand the impor-
tance of the ability to marinate

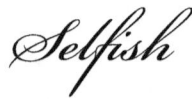

Selfish

I know I got a girl
But I want you and all the special privileges that come with you
My selfishness and pride tells me
You all can be mine, and I expect you to live like that when I know
it's not fine
How can a man decide between two dimes? I keep arguing with
myself
Having to face this decision with time is all that's on mind
On a mission to build an empire; I'll be Lucious Lyon
Pulling you outta binds
I'd do whatever to say you're both mine
I know that's not how this thing seems to be designed
One of you gotta be bad for me; one of you gotta be swine
One of you gotta be wasting my time
But in due time, maybe I'll be selfish, and you both gonna be fine

We Shouldn't Have Never Gave You Money

Niggaz get the first check; instead of putting food on the table,
you go buy a polo and a Rolex, just so you can flex
It's farfetched how far we gotta go in life
Pushing through all the pain and strife
Just to buy small things that look nice
Pedaling through life
We not coming off our dirt bikes
We get muddy, but we still progressing
We come a long way
From being imprisoned on a cotton field
To MJs and Dr. Js doing windmills in Js
To streaming services owned by Beys and Jays
To fashion being dominated
By revolutionaries like Kanye
And they still say

"We should have never gave you niggaz money."

To dominating boxing arenas
Toy boxing with McGregors and Medinas
With young Jean-Michel Basquiats coming out of projects, they
going to have to fear or respect us, rather than continue to neglect
us

Sitting front row at award shows
With Super Bowl goals
With all white and no socks
Women think you're funny and handsome
Like Jamie Foxx
And they still say

"We should have never gave you niggaz money."

I hope we're using the money to escape
Poverty and make hardships stop
That's the all-the-time eating of potty meat, sardines, ramen noo-
dles, bologna, and hot dogs
That's harassing phone calls from bill collectors
That's the rent due on the first but pay by the fifth
We on that *Get Rich or Die Tryin'* like Fif
That's them car notes
That hit us in our throats
That's the ability to save money and stay afloat
That's to ensure our legacies
Have a way to elevate in a world full of hate
Not to stash U-Hauls with money and Warhols
When God call, you can't take it at all
So with only one life to live
When we finally free
I'm sure you can see why we love to ball
You would too if you knocked down
This many walls
But without our struggle
And your misunderstanding

"We should have never gave you niggaz money."

Is probably what you will forever be saying
But the first flaw in that statement is no one just gives you money

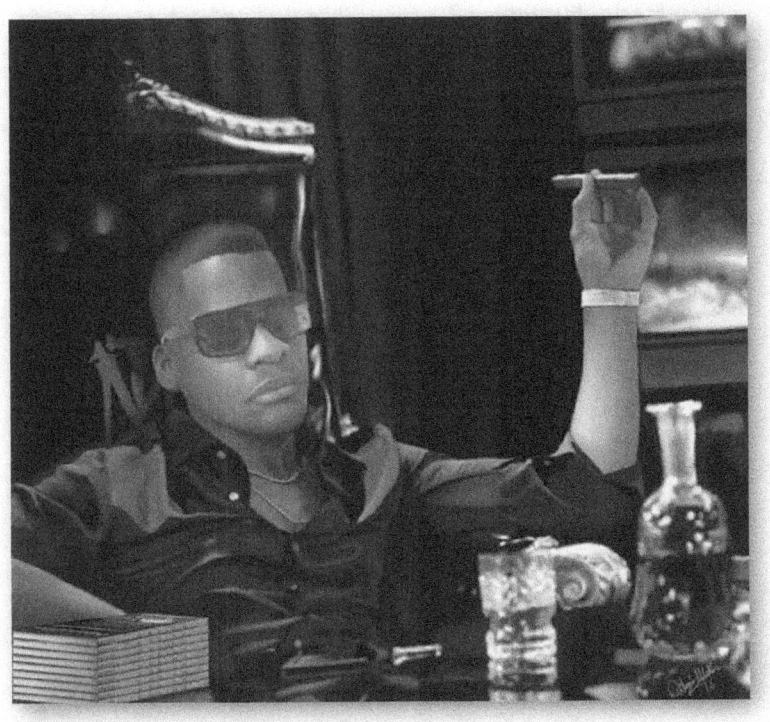

Live, Ace B

Live, Ace B, they'll never love you
You'll never be enough; let's just keep it real, Ace B
I mean, you abandoned your own brother
How can we trust Ace B?
You gotta do better
But you don't necessarily know what to do
You can only seem to see it; you had no help
Just had the faith and the Father; gotta get tougher, Ace B
This ain't back in the days; you not living in the Spike Lee *School Daze*
Cry, Ace B—we know the pain is real
But you can't heal when people never experienced how you feel
You gotta find the truth to help all the youth that look up to you
You got people you love that don't love you
You down on the life—that shit hurts you
You finally outta school; now is your time to rule
I know people backstab you, and all that Pro-Love won't save you
But you got hurt because you showed the true you
You gave them a life raft to stop the sinking without blinking
They gave you hell—fuck they thinking?
Is what you're saying, but if everybody's crazy
You're the one that's sane
You got a sword in your back; imagine how it feels to be betrayed
and sneak attacked
You're becoming great so enemies want to do whatever to not see
you live, Ace B

Let Me Make It Right

I was just fucking them hoes
You don't get a nega back like that
I hear people tell you all the time we will never work
But the truth about that is we together and we not with them
People love to get into your business like they detectives, but they
actually defective
I make mistakes, but I want to be your everything, including
protective
I ask you to let a nigga please make it right
Because without you, I have some lonely nights
I'm handicapped and confused without your vision or sight
Lost in the world because I lost my girl
Lost at sea, searching for treasures and pearls
But now I realize it's all within you, girl

Let me make it right
Let me make it right
I know I fucked up
But I'm trying to do right
Let me make it right
Let me make it right
I'm tired of all the arguing and
I don't wanna fight
You say I stress you out
And keep you up all night

Before we fuss and fight
Baby, give me a chance to make it right
The pressures of losing family
Hits me like war and famine
Out here taking penitentiary chances
Brothers catching cases
Like freshwater salmon
With unfair justice, they slamming doors
And pushing sinners on marble floors
Released and unforgiven
While on world tours
They try to do everything to make it right
Traveling long nights, boarding long flights, chasing visions when
others don't have sight

Betrayal

I sit here a fool because reality has set in
That I would defend and love you to the end
But with realization, I realize you are less of a friend
I feel less of a man because I did everything
I can to be the best man, and you toss me in the trash can for dogs
and low-class men
I'd buy you the latest fashion to keep you beautiful and flashing
Constantly you would get gifts and manis and pedis
Only to break my heart like a New Orleans levy
I'm so embarrassed and humiliated that I even gave you a chance
Great thing I had defense; otherwise, I'd be looking like Rob
Kardashian
I would have killed for you like Smith & Wesson action
But you punish me like Joe Jackson; I could have been your star
like Michael Jackson
You could have been my lady like Freddie Jackson say
But since you're my ex, it's a better day
I feel like you take the man with the most chips like Frito-Lay
When we flexing you call me bae; when I'm down you say we will
talk another day
I know in my heart I have been betrayed; people laugh in my face
when I come around
And I get it—you used me just to get around

And, bruh

Do you ever find it in your heart to pick up the phone and give me a call at all?

Considering I gave a lot of my time helping you reach goals that had nothing to do with me at all

I inherited beef, lost connections, and lost focus on self

Decreases in my wealth in order for your growth in health and wealth

I ask myself, should I have just stayed to my damn self

People only listen for key notes and when they hear your greatness, it's cutthroat

They want your ideas because they see jets and boats

But it will never work because ideas don't generate in the throat

It's from your heart and mind, and in due time we gonna shine

I helped you get on your feet, but if I need help, you got me standing in line or taking a seat

I know it's getting deep; I also know I won't fail

I keep thinking about a cross and some nails

Then I realized that even the King dealt with betrayal

Social Status

From the time we touch the surface of the earth
We find that social status is the most important thing
Most teach us in school to become a part of an organization that contributes to a social point
But the argument at hand is people try so hard to reach a social status
That they forget why they do it or what the impact is
Walking into a hospital, I witnessed a nurse laughing at a weary and sick man
Walking into a police station, I feel hatred and partially see the will of the Ku Klux Klan
Walking into a courtroom, I see lawyers working to prosecute a person
Because their ideals in life aren't of the same cause
Walking into a black community, I see too many thugs and not enough hugs
Listening to music, I hear too much of drugs and not about connection between the spirit and soul
Watching TV and the false commercials say if you pay $9.95 you will be closer to God
The same people who couldn't afford a ride finally find stability and talk recklessly about the lower class, who aren't able
Those who finally get a seat at the table sometimes forget
The voices that shouted them into victory when they were unstable
Point is, social status is something but not everything

Especially if you're not working for the greater good of man
Log on to social media, preferably Facebook, and take a look at how people
Want to contribute to the world
They say things like, "I move that white girl," "I'mma bad bitch," "Real nigga shit,"
"I hate nigger monkeys," "The president is a monkey,"
"I'll bust it open if the money right," "Come on and knock this pussy out like fight night,"
"My baby daddy ain't shit," "Niggaz ain't shit," "Sometimes I hate being black,"
"I'mma go find me a white man," "Niggaz won't treat you right," "Bitches be hating,"
"I'mma fuck her baby daddy just 'cause I can," "I'll be the side chick," "We should both suck his dick,"
"*Man*! I be getting all the hoes," "I'mma paint me a bit from the back,"
"Bitches ain't shit but hoes and tricks," "I want a man who can do everything."
While I sit at home, and bitches be hating
The point is, regardless what we do in life
The energy we give reflects our social status
Truthfully, you may have accomplished many great things
But how you actually apply them to the world is your real status

We All Need a Reason to Smile (Hughes Brothers)

We all need a reason to smile
Some may not be as often, and for some it may take a while, but
surely one day you will smile
Say you lost your job and you can't cut through
But surely one day you will smile when the right one sees you
Your dreams seem unobtainable
But surely one day you will achieve and smile
Your dream man hasn't arrived yet
But surely he will, and you will have a reason too
You struggle for love, and surely one day you will find it
And have a reason to smile
You're living in terrible conditions, not proud of your circum-
stances, faced with intuitions
But one day you will be in a better position and have a reason to
smile
You barely have enough money to pay your bills on time
And you can't sleep because it weighs heavy on your mind
But in due time, you will make it and have a reason to smile
You gave your heart to a scumbag due to his lack of respect; you
live in regret
But when the right one comes, you will smile
You feel like they hate you because you different and they ain't you

Someday someone will see the best in you, and surely you will have a reason to smile
You trusted them, and they let you down; you held them up, and they kicked you down
They drug your name in the dirt, and deeply you were hurt
But when you get up, you will smile
Faced with everyday issues, we tend to not count our blessings
And cry heavy on tissue
Look to the heavens, and he will sort out and assist you
And don't forget to smile

Not Like This

I used to love to see you, but not like this
You were supertalented; you dominated in every sport
Especially on the court—you made seven footers look small
I never imagined at all that I would see you defeated by drugs and
life, which hold you down
You used to be a likeable guy; now they hate you around
We were bad boys who used to run the town
I surely hate how life has taken you down

We were supposed to make it, but not like this
We were supposed to change the world, but not like this
We were supposed to inspire, but not like this
We were gonna live life, *but not like this*!

The shy, pretty girl in school who kept to herself
If trouble went right, you went left, never caring about material-
istic things
While other chicks twerked to be picked up from school by a
hustler
Who bought them chicken wings and Walmart promise rings?
You always did your own thing, focused on progression of your
career
You had a lot of fear and accidentally found comfort in a nightmare
Dating someone you wouldn't dare; I always knew you would find
love, but not like this

Pumping out baby after baby; people telling me you must be crazy
Every year you have a Christmas list, but instead you get his fist
I caught the gist that you try your hardest and he treat you like shit

We were supposed to live our lives, but not like this
We were supposed to make it, but not like this
We were supposed to change the world, but not like this
We were supposed to inspire, but not like this
We were gonna live life, *but not like this*!

You working overtime just trying to cut through
Jeopardizing yourself ultimately to find the best you
Seeking self-improvement, you look for every avenue
Although this is nothing new, you find motivation from those who came before you
Your heart is heavy and you find disconnect from your peers
They stay clouded in mind from drinking beers
While you're battling to find your career
And they're lost in the headlights like deer
You're forgetting you are their biggest fear
While you accelerate, they got their hands on your stick gear
Never being the places you have been, they don't see or hear the man in the mirror
They haven't seen the bright lights and chandeliers
You push every day with hopes that opportunities are near
When it finally appeared, they said you got weird and disappeared
If this is what they say to find justification, then this we adhere
Hated everywhere you go because you search for more
Hated for your heart, thoughts, and skin, but push every day
And you will surely win

We're going to make it, even if it's like this
We're going to change the world, even if it's like this
We're going to inspire, even if it's like this
We're gonna live life, *even if it's like this*!

You Too Little

I unzipped my pants; she said, "You too big."
I unzipped my pants; she said, "You just right."
She said I was too little as we rolled around in my car with no AC
She said I was too little when I couldn't afford to get her hair done
She said I was too little when I couldn't take her out to dinner with her son
She said I was too little when the dope boys came through, riding slow on 24s
She said I was too little when she was starving
And I didn't have money for Skittles
She said I was too little when I couldn't afford Michael Kors and Jimmy Choo
She said I was too little as I broke open the piggy bank for gas money, which she thought was funny
She said I was too little as she let another man get close to her
She said I was too little when the streets swallowed me whole and spit me out
I couldn't afford to do the finer things for her at the time
Because I was caught in the struggle, and being unsympathetic, she even took more advantage
These days I don't know what she's saying because I'm too big to
Pay attention or give an honorable mention to someone with cruel intentions

Faith (Finding Answers in the Heart)

It's all a test of faith, time, and belief
I pray God sends us help
Or relief
Because everyone and everything else sends us obstacles
Just facing adversity
Reconstruction of thoughts
More dangerous than surgery
A young star like Whitney, often
Compared to Sidney Poitier
I just pray God blesses me with an ability to lead people into a better day
I've been holding on for dear life, just trying to live right
I'm driving down long roads with too many red lights
But I somehow know that as long as I keep faith, I will be all right
These dreams keep me up at night
I had these dreams since I had training wheels on my bike
Everywhere I go, people try to stop me, but I keep a will to fight
No matter how much they try to lie
They still can't stop the light
They can't stop faith, wisdom, understanding, and courage
I know some days I will lose focus
I know some days they will feed on me
I know some days I will lose sight of me

I know some days I will be weak in faith
I know some days I will struggle
I know some days won't be safe
I know some days I gotta be brave
I know some days I'm gonna get saved

Machine Gun

I touched down on the map
Keeping my strap; perhaps it's deeper than rap; the beef will get a
bullet in your fitted cap
Let me be great with widgets and apps
Before I put something in your girl gaps
Innovative like the Baps
Running NASCAR laps
Trying to rise from the bottom of the map
While they sleep and take naps
I machine-gun rap
Taking out enemies like Warren Sapp
When we remember Conrad's don't-forget taps
We feign war so we can get into scraps, get you clapped, or get
your whole body wrapped for the love of family and real friends
It's about love, not splurging in a Benz
I'll die for the art that's an ASCAP
Rising as a general, my fingers I snap
And my young boys will give you Ric Flair backslaps after they
tie their bootstraps and chinstraps before they get you entrapped
Suppressing you with mousetraps, shooting out your kneecaps, or
busting you in your lens cap
We get it popping like radiator caps
When we're over, we're never outdone
Enemies sweeter than cinnamon buns
And we hold it down like megatons

While chickens just begun the run
We've been exposed to blowguns
And handguns, but the wordplay will get you done
We live holy like nuns
But occasionally drink and shoot guns like cons; mastered like shoguns, we fear none
Making memories like home runs
Watch what you say when you speak to the don
We lost automachines that used to ride clean like we're the college deans
Hustling for the green while with niggaz like beans; pockets fat in denim jeans
Getting to money is part of the routine
Crime scenes always of nicotine, gas, or lean
Street left me with a heavy heart, even made me mean; you gotta be keen
Ready or not, you know it—you are seen
When you're shining like oil sheen; stay woke, get caffeine; young street teens plotting to put one in your dome and two in your spleen
Finding your body looking aquamarine; the soft get eaten like gelatin
Stay undercover like a submarine, move like a wolverine
Keep your hands clean and have great hygiene and you'll come out strong like polytetrafluorethylene

What Is Black?

What is black?
Black is an alpha color
Which many define as great
When others spit at the taste
Black is beautiful
The only time black isn't beautiful
Is when it's artificial
Like black jelly beans, licorice, and wounded superheroes
Beat and put down by phony zeros
Black, keep ya head up, hero
You see stars only shine in a black night
When I'm thinking of blacks, I think of champions who stayed in
the fight
Like Muhammad Ali, Malcolm X, or Martin Luther King Jr.
Whose roles were crucial and brightened up my black future; the
upcoming and conquering of struggle and depression, changing
lives, leaving progression
I like other colors, but some ain't right
Tormenting and torturing others to be in the light
Not only is black an alpha color or race
It's the color of my face

Didn't Do This

Partially brought into American culture on a slave ship if not already here, and I'm being accused of being violent, but how? I didn't do this

Being lynched, raped, hated, and degraded

We are told we are lowlifes and thugs, but how? We didn't do to any of this

Being sprayed with water hoses

I feel this is just a challenge and somehow proves God has chosen us

I have to wake up every morning to difficult circumstances; rather it's gunshots or thieves trying to run up in my spot

I'm trying hard and giving life everything I got

Been grinding for so long that some days I forgot

I dream big for planes and yachts

And they're doing everything in the world to take my spot

I'm living righteous, but to everyone else I'm juggernaut

I work hard to change my condition, but somehow people manage to get into feelings, but why? I didn't do any of this

I did my part; I paid my bills

Don't hate me because I aspire to do more than Netflix and chill

I'm more into soul-searching and thrills

But I lose motivation when I see young boys being killed

Because they made poor decisions

They got to live with

But I find peace when I can say I had nothing negative to do with this

God Is Everything

Without God, there is no you
Without God, there is no me
Learn our history
And praise God
Praise God
Praise God
Praise God
Praise God!
Without God, how could you stand?
Without God, how could you love?
Praise God
Praise God!
Without God, how could you create?
Without God, how could you prosper?
Praise God!
Without God, how could you live?
Without God, where would you live?
People want to hide the blessing of God, but that's just the enemy
With all your heart, *praise God*!
God is outstanding
God is cool, enormous
God is tremendous
God is wonderful
God is incredible
God is marvelous

God is phenomenal
God is superb
God is magnificent
God is brilliant
God is perfect
God is admirable
God is glorious
God is monumental
God is masterful
God is genuine
God is significant
God is truth
God is colossal
God is wow
God is spectacular
God is impressive
God is vital
God is interesting
God is crucial
God is gigantic
God is powerful
God is massive
God is special
God is mighty
God is meaningful
God is highest
God is almighty
God is earthshaking
God is groundbreaking

God is superhero
God is superpower
God is giant
God is elevated
God is general
God is everything
God gives me the passion to write; God gives me direction
God saved me from hardships
God made a way for me when there was no way
I will never forget what God has done for me
I will never forget what God has for me
I will never stop believing in God
All my life I have been told about the greatness of God
I think it's about time that I start to learn a little bit more about
God
Amen

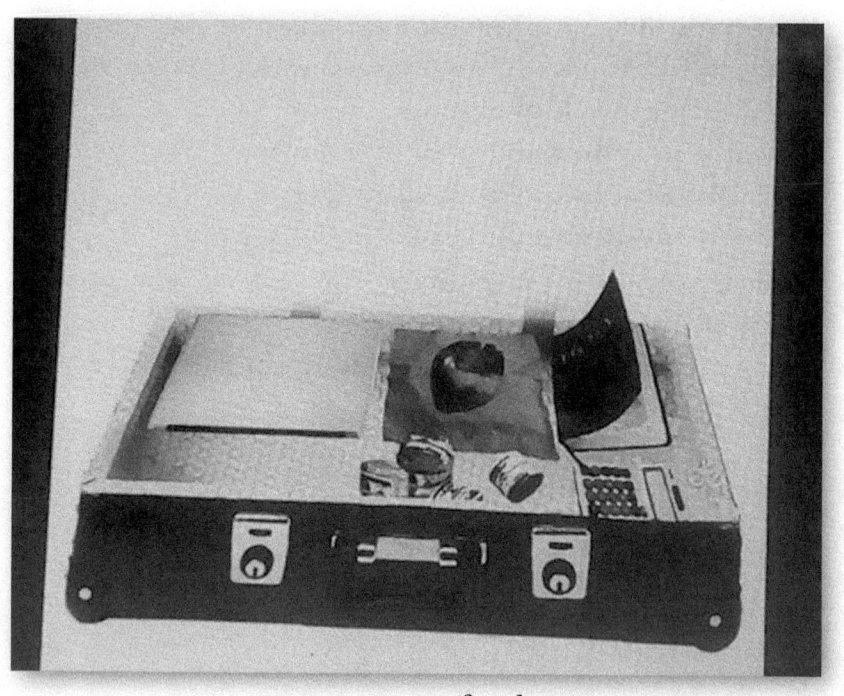

www.truewarriorfamily.com
www.youtube.com/acebmartin

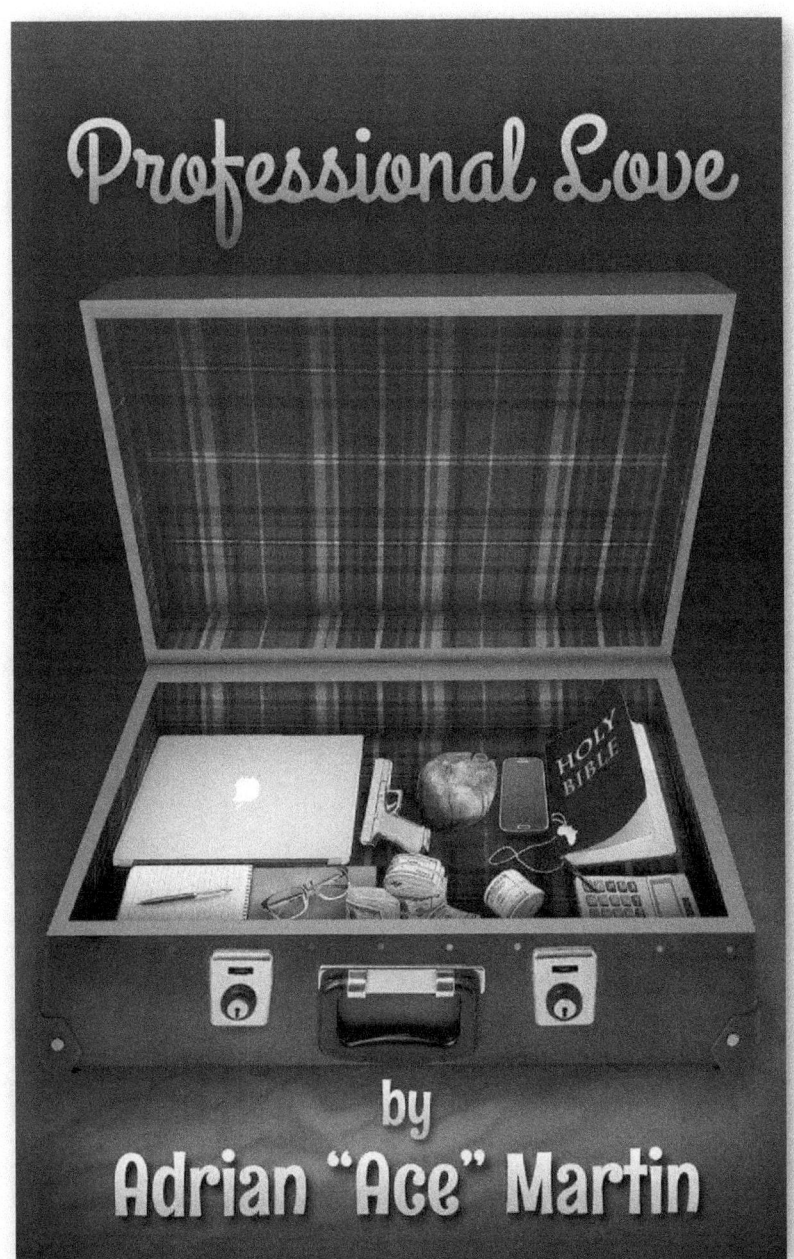

It is available everywhere

www.ingramcontent.com/pod-product-compliance
Lightning Source LLC
Chambersburg PA
CBHW072231170526
45158CB00002BA/849